THE STORY STARTS OUT WAY BEFORE I EVEN KNEW HIM.

HIS STORY HAS BEEN RETOLD...

BACKWARDS...

AND FORWARDS...

SIDE-TO-SIDE,

INSIDE OUT

AND EVEN BOTTOM TO TOP.

SAD THING IS... THAT'S HOW SHAWN WOULD SEE THINGS ON THE WRITTEN PAGE.

BACKWARDS?

... BACKWARDS, LIKE WITH THE LETTERS B AND D.

WANT TO GO TO-- WAIT...

THIS IS YOUR CLASS?

UH... ACTUALLY, NAH!

I'M DOWN THE HALL, MAN. C'MON!

BEFORE ARRIVING INTO HIS SEVENTH-GRADE SPECIAL EDUCATION CLASSROOM, SHAWN WAS MISBEHAVING IN THE HALLWAY WITH HIS FRIEND.

THE FIRST THREE STUDENTS HAD COMPLETED READING AND SHAWN'S BLOOD PRESSURE CONTINUED TO RISE. AS HIS TURN WAS GETTING CLOSER, ALL HE THOUGHT ABOUT WAS HIS ESCAPE. HE WANTED TO BE SAVED.

AS HIS TURN APPROACHED, SHAWN COULD NOT UNDERSTAND WHAT WAS BEING READ, AND HOW THE PASSAGES IN THE BOOK WERE LINKED. WHILE HE WAS WAITING HIS TURN SHAWN PRACTICED READING AND REREADING THE PASSAGE TO MAKE SURE HE DID NOT SOUND STUPID.

SHAWN WAS BEING ATTACKED FROM BOTH ANXIETY AND DYSLEXIA.

SHAWN!

"GO TO THE OFFICE!"

SHAWN HAD SAVED HIMSELF BY GETTING REMOVED FROM CLASS.

FAST FORWARD...

SHAWN'S FRUSTRATION CONTINUED...

IN HIGH SCHOOL, HE FELT HOPELESS, AND WAS IN CONSTANT TROUBLE.

NO ADULT WAS TEACHING HIM HOW TO READ.

DESPITE HIS ACADEMIC OBSTACLES, HE BECAME A PEER MENTOR WITH THE SPECIAL OLYMPICS PROGRAM.

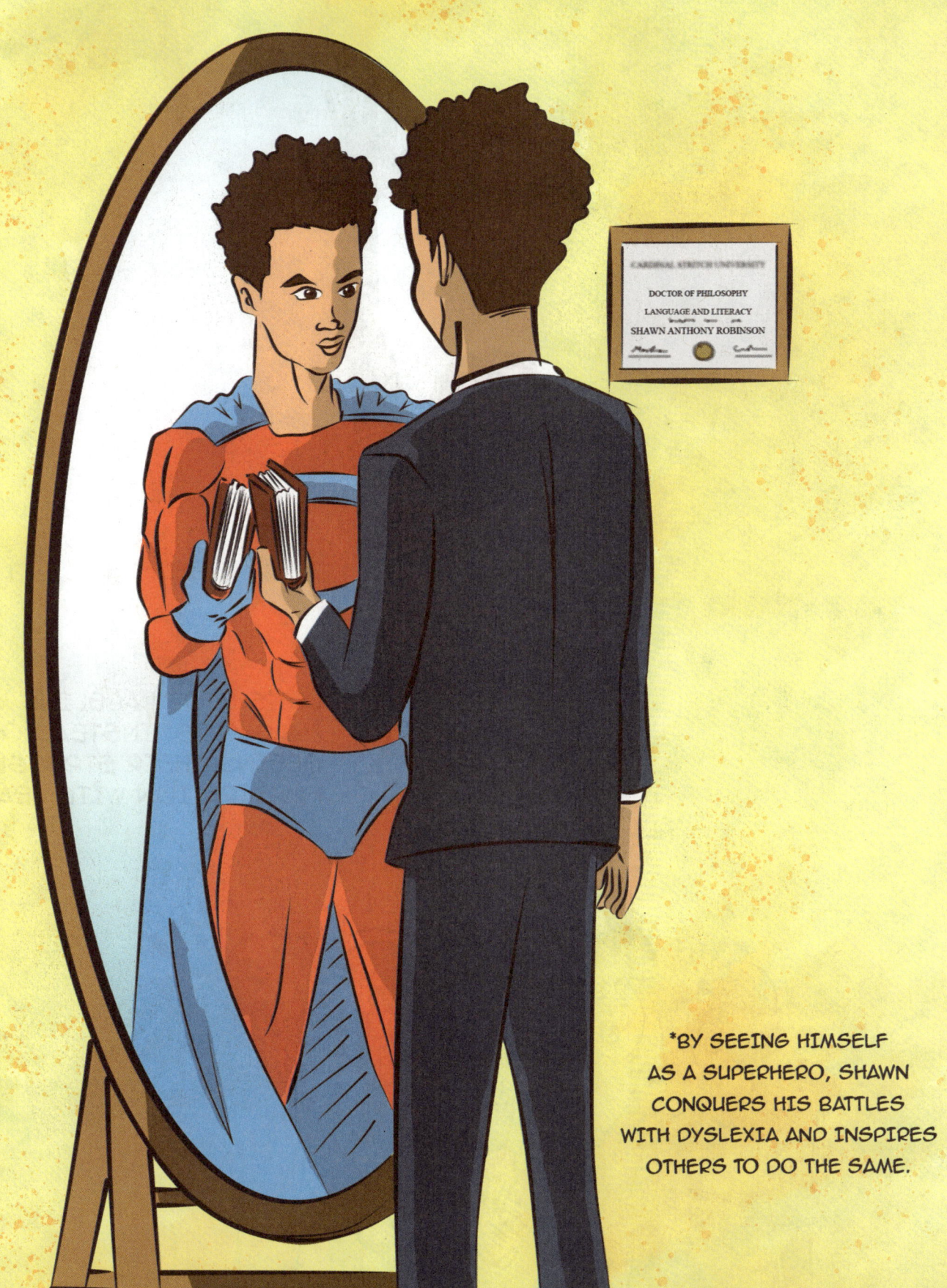

BY THE WAY, WITH ALL THE STUFF GOING ON IN HIS STORY, I FORGOT TO INTRODUCE MYSELF TO YOU.

MY NAME IS JEREMIAH, AND I DON'T JUST CALL HIM DOCTOR SHAWN ANTHONY ROBINSON DYSLEXIA DUDE...

I CALL HIM

DAD.

BIOGRAPHY

Authors

Shawn Anthony Robinson, Ph.D.

Shawn Anthony Robinson Ph.D. is a Senior Research Associate in the Wisconsin's Equity and Inclusion Laboratory (Wei LAB) at the University of Wisconsin-Madison, an author, a dyslexia consultant, and serves on the Board of Directors with the International Dyslexia Association. Robinson graduated from the University of Wisconsin Oshkosh (UWO) with a Bachelors of Science in Human Services, a Master's in Education from DePaul University, and a PhD in Language and Literacy from Cardinal Stritch University. Robinson has received several distinguished honors throughout his early career such as: the 2017 Alumni Achievement Award/New Trier High School Alumni Hall of Honor; the 2016 Outstanding Young Alumni Award from UWO; served as a fellow for the 2015 8th Annual Asa G. Hilliard III and Barbara A. Sizemore Research Institute on African Americans and Education – American Educational Research Association; and the 2013 Achievement Gap Institute – Vanderbilt University Peabody College of Education & Human Development; and the All-State Insurance's 2005 Educator. Robinson is also a Life Member of Alpha Phi Alpha Fraternity, Inc.

Inshirah Robinson

Inshirah Robinson is a proud wife and mother of two boys, Jeremiah and Ezekiel, who are the light of her life. She is currently a graduate student in the Doctorate of Nurse Practitioner Certified Registered Nurse Anesthetist program at the University of Wisconsin Oshkosh. She holds a Bachelors of Science in Nursing Cum Laude from the University of Wisconsin – Oshkosh and a Bachelor of Business Administration, 2006 Loyola University Chicago.

Illustrator, Graphic Artist

Brandon Hadnot-Walker

Brandon Hadnot-Walker, born December 3, 1988, is a Milwaukee, WI native living in Orlando, FL as a Graphic Designer and Filmmaker. As the son of the late Theresa Hilber, who was a local Community Organizer, Small Business owner, and Designer, he is heavily influenced by the way she infused her personal passions into her work and public speeches. Since graduating with a Bachelor of Arts degree in Media Arts and Game Development at the University of Wisconsin-Whitewater in 2011, he has been an independent professional Designer for nearly a full decade. Currently, Brandon teaches Graphic Design & Web Development in a small classroom in hopes to build the next generation of Creatives who design with their hearts first. His involvement in illustrating Doctor Dyslexia Dude is rooted in his friendship and previous creative collaborations with Dr. Shawn Anthony Robinson, PhD. spanning his years in undergrad.